T0152206

BOOKS BY JULIEN POIRIER

El Golpe Chileño (Ugly Duckling Presse, 2010)

Way Too West (Bootstrap Press, 2015)

OUT OF PRINT

CITY LIGHTS SPOTLIGHT SERIES NO. 14

JULIEN POIRIER

OUT OF PRINT

CITY LIGHTS

SAN FRANCISCO

CITY LIGHTS SPOTLIGHT

The City Lights Spotlight Series was founded in 2009,
and is edited by Garrett Caples.

Library of Congress Cataloging-in-Publication Data
Names: Poirier, Julien, author.
Title: Out of print / Julien Poirier.
Description: San Francisco : City Lights Publishers, [2016] | Series: City Lights spotlight ; 14
Identifiers: LCCN 2015042171 | ISBN 9780872867048 (softcover)
Subjects: | BISAC: POETRY / American / General.
| LITERARY COLLECTIONS /
American / General. | POLITICAL SCIENCE / Civics & Citizenship.
Classification: LCC PS3616.O5465 A6 2016 | DDC 811/.6—dc23
LC record available at http://lccn.loc.gov/2015042171

ACKNOWLEDGMENTS

Some of these poems first appeared in print in *Try!*, *New York Nights*, *The Brooklyn Rail*, *Where Eagles Dare*, *Poems by Sunday* and *Night Palace*; online at *Harriet* and *Puppyflowers*; in the chapbook *Absurd Good News* (Insert Blanc Press, 2006); and in *POETBOOK #6*, an artist book illuminated by Brian Lucas. Thanks to Naima Ezana for fixing the French on "Mouche Verte Morte."

All City Lights Books are distributed to the trade by
Consortium Book Sales and Distribution: www.cbsd.com

For small press poetry titles by this author and others,
visit Small Press Distribution: www.spdbooks.com

City Lights Books are published at the City Lights Bookstore,
261 Columbus Avenue, San Francisco, CA 94133
www.citylights.com

CONTENTS

Opening Poem 1

17 Reasons Why 2

Average Past 4

Dear Reader 5

Back on Rooster 6

Poem ("I used to be the biggest leftist") 7

The 2nd Amendment Never Sleeps 9

Pepper's Ghost 12

Entropy Rex 14

Shimmering Lucifers 19

Stage 4 Lung Cancer Won't Wait 21

Showdown with Death 23

The Baboon Is Eating Strawberries 25

Great Escapes in New York City 26

Investigation 32

Winnemucca 34

Four Failed Revolutions 38

"When I was growing up in America" 42

Orchestre de Paris 44
Louis Armstrong 46
The 1906 San Francisco Earthquake and Fire (An Episode) 48
That's What I'm Saying 50
Drunkard's Almanac 56
Existentialist Spa 58
Gardens & Airplanes 60
The Commodity Sings to Its Beloved 62
Heavy Losses, Boss 66
Egyptian Bowling Trophy 71
There's Love and Then There's Love 73
Zero with a Thousand Aces 76
Move On 79
Inner Oaf 80
Pierre de Ronsard 82
The Perfect Man 84
The Red Caps 86
Mouche Verte Morte 88
Green Bottle Fly 89
Louis Armstrong International 92
Berkeley Voice Notes 94

Independently Blue 100
If You're Reading This 101
Real-Life Adventure 103
This Is the Life 104
Silver to Silver 106

OUT OF PRINT

OPENING POEM

Kailey,
All my poems are for you
Read 'em all the livelong day
Naked as a horse
I mean, naked ON a horse
Don't mind
The paintballers
Zombies on the drag race course
You're wind, you melt on my tongue
News anchor ax murderer
Nun
With bong-hit eyes
The great city this crater once was
No one can touch you
Not a fleck of spattered brain
On your cucumber 3-piece
You and me, you and me
Till the pine cones turn
Insane.

17 REASONS WHY

First
I went to the second-hand store
to pick up some second-hand smoke
but smoke got in my third eye
on the 4th of July
while I drank a fifth of rye
to myself for the sixth
time since my seventh
birthday.
By eight I was lit to the
nines
but not one tenth of me
wanted to go back to 11th St.
where you and your twelve baby brothers
were baking
Friday the 13th cookies
for their fourteen freeloading
Fifteen Day Adventist sixteen-
candle-looking girlfriends
with *Seventeen* magazine subscriptions

and eighteen burning draft cards
in nineteen takes on a backlot
at 20th Century-Fox.
The 21st Century started
on September 11th
and was over in twenty seconds,
and September 23rd is the vernal equinox
on Machu Picchu.
24 hours in a day
25 cents to play.

AVERAGE PAST

you add up our youths
and cut it in half
that's how you arrive at the average past
nice place
no one on the bridge
many a bottle
more swallows than Capistrano
now the standard median you
has one leg
a tipped-off glass eye
and a mean disposition
toward a 20th-Century bum like me
but fuck if
I'd rather be here than there
getting burned in your arms
to android zydeco

Dear Reader, among the many things I enjoy
is your beautiful voice. I have stared
into your eyes, and found no fear there.
The strains of a jolting wonderful fuck
fill our airshaft, and you smile. Nearly
to yourself, but I detect every subtle change
on your noble and open face, just as the whorls
on your fingertips rock me gently like waves.
Your mind is as unpredictable as your ear
is absolute, and your taste (if it's a matter
of taste) is peerless. I have lived with you
now, for so long the stars have begun
to glint along mountains even as my hand
trails through the stream: Here, drink
before it runs through my fingers, before
it changes its ways, though you know
nothing is ever lost, in your wisdom
wild as silence.

BACK ON ROOSTER

Stop your wicked ways
Ye stragglers and ye thieves
Open up your cobra vest
Feed your chicken fees
The sun is risking rising now
Its hands are rupee rich
Your rooster's on a funky mission
To crow zero emissions
And span the fiscal stars
Whose stucco mansion fief
On solitudinal seed
Zips up fountains like snow peas
All along the lone cuneiverse
Bathers in their phases on leashes
Chase moons to salt traces
Bait capers with bootleg toothpaste
Diamonds on the river
When saxophones rock steady
From the tip of the past
To the back of the hand

POEM

I used to be the biggest leftist
till I started finding money on the street

    became the Invisible Hand

warily
tinfoiling a burrito at the hippest taqueria
in Jerusalem

devouring
the authoritative pupa
            of Watergate

What's this Watergate?
fuggetaboudit!

it's not your day job
to digest the 20th Century

I bring you only the most scintillating gallstones,

Dr. Wei (UCSF)
photographed them
with the same love
he kept
for bison and ghost barns
of flute-silver knots
and
their platforms

made T-Rex look like IT

THE 2ND AMENDMENT NEVER SLEEPS

On July 4th
we celebrate
the day we all kicked ourselves
out of the country
out of
one major novel
from the postwar boom
after another
into this
crazy poem three million
billion lines long and
counting and no end
or point   in sight

and I say—of course
America is nothing
but one big car park, hot enough
to put blisters on your bare teeth
ranged
by the maddest most longest sustained

carnival in history
an inchoate
crowning of purple
hummingbird pitbulls
thwipping
carwash kelp
aviator shades
hotwired
by the naked hardbody
of a supermoon
of a sun
that means to destroy us
sexually with perfect
discipline—and

the total loss of jungle
crosses with swastikas fried
in ashcans of honey
aquamarine
sharkfins split the rockers
from the breakers
but really
everyone is all mixed up

thrown together
and subject
to the same big rip off

and it's great
it's just great

7-4-15

PEPPER'S GHOST

I know your planet is about to be
enrobed in fire, and I'm trying hard to care.

I know we're the same—were even in bed
with the same woman once
(though on your planet
she looked like a 60-foot
birch tree w/
telepathic ankles)

I know a version of the peach
drops there
and that your parks are holes
in the 4th wall
of your hole-in-the-wall
Chicagos.

We might be
the best friends to have never
talked

more like pieces of the same
chromosome mercury
hammered across space.

Your kids, your crazy hang-ups
and records you never play
but will never sell . . . am I just seeing my own face
shaving on the earthless sky?

gah! this is the last day
. . . don't try to see it out,
              no one
will survive, not a single one.

ENTROPY REX

Ever get all het up
for the express purpose
of storming out of the whole spectacle?
as if to achieve *proper escape velocity*
from the culture you need
to turn your brain into a collage
of the gladiators' vinyl capes
then light it on fire—
propelling a cigarette paper
rocketship from Moscow
to certain but totally
worth-it death
in a virtually wordless vacuum?
A sense of self
turns out not to be
so essential after all
when
anybody at any moment could
be hit with such trauma
it would immobilize

or mutate you forever
the Santa hat
with the white rabbit
in the wrong place
turn the dream
you into a Manchurian Candidate
in the empire of dreams—
where do it
+ Hollywood
cross?

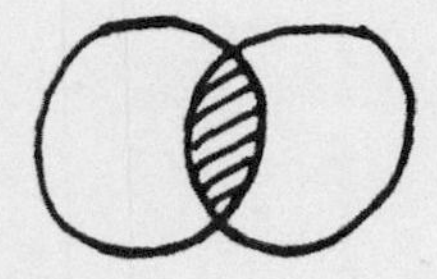

and who
are the hygienists of the
DEEP STATE of that
empire and what
is their agenda?
Blah.
They are so *vapid* and *insipid* these career AL-

PHAS masquerading as Black
Friday campers in a kind of masochistic
Saturnalia—
their money it was
that turned ENTROPY into a talkie
and ever since
there's been only 5 ways to die.
Or was it 4?
Buncha creeps . . .
And I'm regaled by their Picassos
on the way to the bathroom
at the big party
in the big producer's ranch house I emerge from
the bamboo rushes to crash—
So?
I wonder if I'm doing it again,
making it all up, dramatizing
a conflict that
doesn't need me, one
that is really an inter-
play of forces fucking
each other into
mutual destruction

ecstatically,
and all I can make of it
all I can make stick
in my excited confusion, is this
political thriller—
O FUDGE! Neolithic.
What would it mean
to disengage
to truly draw a blank
when you
outline the end for me
—and stare ahead
with yawning eyes,
limpid with stupidity?
That's an ignorance you've got to earn,
though some are born to it
I'm told. I think I'm not as good
as most Americans
at splitting hairs.
No beheaded journalist
haunts this 4th of July campsite,
just pale smoke
and bike bells

a green frisbee and boys' voices
that haven't changed yet.
The cities feel tropical at this
remove, the great
American cities you have to pass through
suburbs to get to, in some cases
spending your entire adolescence there.
Or is this
all that's left,
Self,
after the twin hydraulic blasts
of the death of your parents
and the defection of your kids
tear you a new one,
and you're selling cat trees
on the side of the road?

SHIMMERING LUCIFERS

Four square monks drive a Coupe de Ville
Through the vale, over the hill

To get to where the savings are,
They square their shoulders and point the car

They bang their heads when the radio blares
That song about the lady who bought the stairs

And the dandy in back swirls down the chrome handle
To cast weird sun on his pilgrim sandal

Where tokens once slurried to a buttercup Hajj
What now? O shimmering mercantile Alcatraz!

Mobius ministries fringe the haze
Of toothbrush choirs in a Yangtze glaze

Foaming in pollens of this lobotomized valley
Ever since Yankee Candle broke up Bee's Alley

Where skanking confederates
Did trail natty satins, debt

Free, and Sanity herself
(Now a scent, top-shelf)

Administered to gutter pirate queens
Mini homecomings woven on the cosmic screen

And whispered in a turtle's ear,
Kid monk you dream, it was the beer

You vowed to brew
Just like the thread will lose its screw

Just like the brain will shed its wrinkles,
Diverting shipwreck's periwinkles

To be reborn in a lonely place,
Truth's best conducted by an unclaimed face

STAGE 4 LUNG CANCER WON'T WAIT

Untenable
—that's the word I'm after
but if it brings you
pleasure, my dear
I'm all for it—
though we can't afford to live
in this city
we can always gad about
in books
picked for portability—the soul
of discretion is
a bit dotty,
tall tale of the afterlife
it hardly embellishes
on the edible mandala we all smell rising—
abandon
me in the bubbling shadows
with my myopic m'stash
Seriously?

Me too—about habit
I'm avidly ritualistic
and *exactly*
like everyone who's ever lived,
bringing our best
every fucking day
synchronized
on the oilslick of interchangeable animal forms
to look like we're losing it
alone.

SHOWDOWN WITH DEATH

Who's ready for a showdown with death?
Who's wiretapping the silent majority?
Who's ready to start the War on Death?
Who's ready to tell the men from the boys?
Who's ready to tear the baby from the womb?
Who's going to hit death from the air?
Who's going to hit death from the sea?
Who's going to hide money under death's pillow?
Who's going to breastfeed death?
Who's going to give death a cigarette?
Who's going to bug him till he quits?
Who will mother death?
Who will father death?
Who will smother death?
Who will kill death with a kiss?
Who will give death everything he ever wanted?
Who will kidnap death?
Who will abandon death in a huge city and see what happens?
Who's ready for a showdown with death?
Who's ready to stand face to face, mingle breath?

Who's ready to mime death?
Who's ready to call him a has-been?
Boss-man?
Orangutan-fucker?
Who's going to pay for the comeback?
Who's going to put death in the hole?
Who's going to whip him with car antenna, tase death?
Who's going to follow death to the ends of the earth?
Who's going to send death the top joint of his pinky in a box of
chocolates?
Who's going to drive death to the border?
Who's going to kick down death's door?
Who's going to breathe heavy into his phone?
Who will pinch his nose when he snores?
Who will watch him as he sleeps and remember how he used to be?
Who will hide the knives?
Who will ice the cake?

THE BABOON IS EATING STRAWBERRIES

The baboon is eating strawberries
expired on the shelf
of the Ft. Bragg Safeway.
A coastal landscape
with waves
like inexpertly torn tinfoil hangs
above his left shoulder
at the check-in desk
of an abandoned motel.
The ocean itself
is only a sound
through the torn window screen
where some hardscrabble bush
about to flower
is just a smell.
Will something appropriately
random please
happen to convince me
reality is still playing
with a full deck?

GREAT ESCAPES IN NEW YORK CITY

FOR FILIP MARINOVICH

Rockefeller Plaza Madison Square Garden the Carnegie Hall
and its toy Chow, the Carnegie Delicatessen
"Delicatessen"
being a quintessentially New York word
"*Je parle newyorkais,*" you could say.
I lived there for 13 years, more in than out of
love—13 years
= a lot of Jewish rye,
brown mustard,
fat pickles in cloudy brine,
cheese full of holes.
It's a city where Douglas Fairbanks Jr., the dashing actor
of Sinbad fame, can die
as I'm eating ice cream in bed
watching Douglas Fairbanks Jr.
in *Sinbad the Sailor*—
and you can read all about it in the morning *Post*,
that candy cane dipped in Raid

—a city
where King Kong peers into the penthouse
of a replica Empire State
to find out how blondes tick.
When I was a young man
I would stand on Broadway in pinstripe pants and a tank top,
talking to Ben who had
back then, green hair,
about what movie we should see
to beat the heat.
Pete was in his apartment right upstairs
but we weren't best friends yet,
we hadn't even met.
New York is a city where you can drop acid,
put on a green-thumb floppy hat and glasses,
sit on the bench
in Tompkins Square Park after walking
120 blocks, every spot taken,
tripping with strangers who are possibly secret
giants of jazz.
Topaz obsidian tourmaline diamond stylus
nothing's so lovely as hot coals and the New York City skyline
is a bonfire, a bonfire in a mirror

pouring through your fingers.
New York New York has the big museums cool it costs
a quarter all day I always
visit Vermeer's psychedelic
Persian rug painting and the stolen mummies, hit the
drinking fountain, snow mo-
ney, maybe go see the harp-
sichord inlaid with cloudy
silver shims and real ebony
bush league keys
like a rookie safe breaker in waterlily scrubs
—cut across the Park at 81st for a rare burger and
fountain Coke with lemon
slice and ice roulette in amber plastic glass,
American.
Re-reading *Franny and Zooey* now
or lamenting the descent of the *Voice*,
even my political dissent is USDA Choice,
I Bogart
Bacall's still lips
—I'm that sure our side will win,
I'm serving
fried tennis balls rolled in powdered sugar

to the vanguard—Albert Ayler
niçoise on tent city
golf links with home fries,
Ask Abby catsup and waffles.
The alluvial silver swirls every time someone opens a door
at the frat house, now occupied by upper-middle-class freak whiz
  kids,
the paint is still wet on their banners.
I've never met most any of these people
who seem to come from underground shores
to kneel at Gena's desk in the dark.
It's hard not to spin out revolutionary scenarios,
beer is one cure for doctrinaire amplifications,
revolution is a sitting duck for planned obsolescence
saturating the market in voice recognition,
I'd just as soon talk to God,
Caliphs with box beards with Martian bedside manners aspiring to
  translate chaos
into the corpse of chaos.
Nevertheless I consider myself a revolutionary,
a grunt revolutionary at times a reserve revolutionary
although I don't know who's Comandante, I think
some group brain, big enough to contain the spread

of counter-revolutionary flatware zooming through space
with its voodoo doll scorpion,
space in which this brain is the last potato chip
and the astronaut's gloves
bump up against the roses in the rose garden,
but the breakers of ancient codes reveal this to be a symbol for
scalping:
We're lucky to be walking together through this city of bridges,
too bad luck is worthless
in the face of the horror it cultivates
elsewhere, luckily.
I don't want to die!
What about my wife and daughter and unborn son or daughter?
I don't want to forget I ever wrote this.
One of the things I do is sit around writing down things that take
place in my mind.
It's not what you would call a living, but I've lived by writing for a
long time.
It's a habit, a very deep habit I think I may be able to break by writ-
ing more.
It's how I theatricalize an identity crisis
that I trust is universal.
It's role reversal with you if you are in.

My speechless confusion is apparently inadequate
because I've got a bad habit for taking a stab at
the very very abstract and recondite.
I admit the purely mechanical appeals to me,
I'm actually trying to write the organic equivalent
here, to be natural with my pencil and allow the naturally
occurring minerals to embed alphabetically.
New York trains run all night,
lost peacock feather of the *Post* under orange seat
in harmonica cars,
graveyard shifters nodding home
—their solidity is only an outward show,
really they're snowmen with no more eyes,
cheeks still glowing from the imploding towers.
Stoner snowmen
the ghosts of oysters are your kneepads
while you crawl the sewers with Sinbad
looking for your button nose.

INVESTIGATION

A thousand poets are working together
on the same great poem but they don't know it
yet, only you and I can make this obvious
—and many of my favorite are alive to this compulsion
though their practice demands a temporary, however
longterm deflection of the obvious—to them
by staying in our skins, which will soon
reel with fast crazy lightshows of their breaking
travels, faces flung up from the interior
of a huge wilderness—bloody mirror of the universe
as if our skins were newsreels wrapping bone and jetpink blubber,
rattling off escapades and breathless descents
onto potentially hostile moons of the liver
the esophagus a milkshake straw to the disembodied
the damned and the zoologically bussed—we invite this
by staying in our skins, Void Frontiers
full up, not a hatless atom unenlisted
in the tail-eating, which we reached and where
we'll rot, nothing wrong with that, each of us
in a kind of private self-enclosed BIG BANG, the same

for everything that lives, at that instant only
thereafter harmonically surfaced to warp
on the chaotic level, the universe having been pegged
a bright black balloon, a beanstalk I would say
or a long-playing record that never stops playing
so you are always there when the needle drops.
But any elaboration of a detail, by experience
would start out being generally familiar to everyone
listening, but the more you go into it the more
people leave, not out of spite, because
remember everyone's talking at once, but because this exchange
        is an investigation
into understanding—that's how it started
and that's its purpose, to find out
where it stops happening.

WINNEMUCCA

The first thing you've got to understand
is that poetry changed my life
so you might think of it
as just something you do
like a hobby or even a passion
or even like mudwrestling
a buff male stripper
in a bar in Winnemucca
where they blare outright racist country music
unlike anything you've ever heard
even in America, and you're so stoned
you can't move
you're undergoing
a total species transformation
right there in the mud—
but I think of it, writing poetry, as a way of changing
the world: and this is what I mean

I mean
it changes the world the same way a bug

getting born changes the
dirty or a man getting a haircut
looks more pretty
or a book missing pages is a little
lighter
it's just a way of making your good friends tighter
a way of peeling potatoes
steaming ladles
shining buckles and catching cusses
all the way out to the beach at night
to me
poetry is like a thrown, like a solid cold thrown
it's a way of bringing joy and befuddlement
so
I can't be too careful
choosing my words
since they come
straight out of your mouth
at least that's what I'm going for

I understand you don't really understand
why poetry obsesses so many people
why there are so many poets today writing poetry

well all I can say is it really gets you
it gets you down in your kid guts
and you think about how maybe there could be a big
kid joy
patty, like the opposite of the communist patty
or of fat apocryphal capitalists selling pharmaceuticals in Africa
which despite their apocryphacality EXIST, I Met One
he was hitting on me
he was kind and rich and would have took me all the way
down to Fez and put me up in a nice comfortable hotel
with clean crisp pillow cases and Moroccan chicken eggs
every morning with dates and orangutan juice
squeezed right before your eyes
a nice big party of the unaffiliated
backward walking doe
with laser tags piercing their ears and
rusting

it'll take all night to tell you how much I hope you come along
the event will be OVER by the time I convince you
or you'll go alone
leave me rhapsodizing in this little moldy apartment
in my hometown

I'll get to you soon
I'll get to how sexy you are as an old person
and how wise you are as a cheerleader
gaslighting the limo skyroof
how your skin keeps changing from black to white
and your eyes keep crossing
the Khyber Pass
and the Bering Strait
and slaughtering big dumb bear-things on sight
and gathering up the fat silver salmons
in nets
and radiating to the jewel necklaces of caves
and thigh bones on broken tanning beds
and your hands keep chopping birds' faces into trees
I'll get to you
in just a sec!

but first I want you to taste this jam
and tell me if it's not delicious
you don't even want to see the flying crabs that live on this island
Isla de los Hijos de las Mujeres de las Albas Eternas

FOUR FAILED REVOLUTIONS

Whatcha doin'?

The less you know about it, kid, the better.

Aw, c'mon mister.

I'm writing poetry.

Hey, I've heard of that. . . . Are you a fruit or something?

Not exactly. I'm here to bring down the State.

What do you mean, like the State of California?

The State of California will have to recognize me as its new supreme ruler.

Wow, what's that, like Shakespeare or something?

*

Hey, what are you doing?

Writing a poem.

Why? No one reads poetry anymore.

This poem means to change all that.

How does that work if no one will even read it?

When I am the Ayatollah of Burbank, they'll have to do more than just read it.

*

Hey, what's going on?

Just a moment.

What are you working on there?

What does it look like I'm working on? Will you just—?

OK, take it easy buddy. I can see you're working on a recipe.

(Putting down pencil and glaring at interlocutor) It is a recipe of sorts. It's a recipe for the overthrow of the State. In the form of a poem.

I don't want to eat that.

*

Hey, what are you up to there?

Oh, just polishing up this poem I've been working on.

Oh, wow! I'd love to read it, when it's ready.

It's ready right now.

(The next day)

So what did you think?

Well. Wow, I mean, so interesting. I don't think I've ever read anything quite like it. I don't know if I *got* everything. I have to admit, I didn't finish . . . I fell asleep with it in my hands. But the crazy thing is, I had this dream, this amazing dream where I was walking through this pulsing astral kaleidoscope, and there was this *music*—and it was perfectly clear to me, like a revelation, like a *teaching* I was carrying, that we—people, I mean all of us—need to create a new language, a new living language to subvert the State—to delegitimize its authority.

Really?

Yeah. I don't know *where* that came from.

Or maybe not to subvert the State. Maybe more like: to convince the State to come up with some money to help publish my book.

When I was growing up in America there was always one president who I had a particular liking for. Every day I would visit him down in the meadow and speak softly to him and shave his face. I would feed him little chunks of steak and tiny glasses of brandy—the President would take the food right out of my fingers.

One day my father told me were we going to have to kill the President. I really lost it—I wept and threw myself at my father and pounded him with my fists, but he said we had no choice. Raising and slaughtering presidents was his job, and we had to eat.

At first I didn't want to watch, but in the end I decided to accompany my father to the meadow the next morning. The President was standing in the tall grass with frost on his wrinkled suit. My father took the President gently by the wrist and inserted a needle into the vein on the inner-elbow of his right arm. The President's eyes instantly expanded and grew watery and he folded onto the grass. My father removed a hacksaw from his belt as I wept. He sawed the President's head off—dark blood flowed into the stiff white grass—and lifted the President's limp left hand. He explained to me that a president's ring finger was considered a particular delicacy in town, and neatly severed the finger from the palm just below the ring.

ORCHESTRE DE PARIS

They put the Orchestre de Paris up in neon,
a pretty violet neon reflecting
the perfect goatee, a limousine
on a black shoe, a romantic pirate. As a woman
I would blow this pirate in the tropical sand,
his being a scheme of beard
and scimitar scar.
But the most thrilling arrangements
turn boring,
life must remain di-
verse,
the fortune you make is there to lose.
One night at the opera in coral tiara, by morning
rags with a shopping bag.
Like that famous beauty who stood by her man
long after he was bones,
and ran his fallow coalmine single-handed.
And then returned to Kansas City with broken eyes
and looks violently rubbed out,
to be shunned by the top society,

sneered at,
standing on nothing but her love for a man so long dead
he had become a child in her mind.
I would like, and expect
to lose like she did, once so beautiful.
I hope I have the courage to stand with the lost,
the broken and the mad.
Put out the eyes of your parakeets.

LOUIS ARMSTRONG

Louis Armstrong, best trumpet ever
ate at Louis Cairo's
with Humphrey Bogart
Detroit Oysters
the Sebastian Bachs ("fuck
this lousy inferior grub") and hauled out
across the great American road
dead serious
an affront to historians
the followers of St. Francis
whose kits may lapse
but who are never off the spring
you can smell it on them
cocktail sauce
double whiskeys halfprice
their eyes shock you, it's a real shock
even if you know
lip split in two
on soft brass
copper harpoon in a solution

of creeping pink
otherworldly ash
ebbing on the seafloor

THE 1906 SAN FRANCISCO EARTHQUAKE AND FIRE (AN EPISODE)

From here accounts conflict, but 4
Chinese valets
remember Barrymore leaving
the hotel alone
to drink. But Caruso was driven mad
there, and clutched his portrait
of Roosevelt "close
to tears"
surrounded by Caruso
"close to tears"
the portrait in his hand.
And Barrymore
drinking alone, parting the flames
anything to repair . . . any excuse . . .
while an undertaker
blazed in his storefront, meticulously
polishing coffin handles
and a flamingo
flagged through

the smoke hardly noted
by the mad tenor, who mumbled
just then (I'm guessing)
"I want my sketchpad"

THAT'S WHAT I'M SAYING

Well it's evening, fishily

and the moon is full, what a day! and in your face

over Clement Pho.

A few of us are going out tonight, taking a page from the moon.

It's warming the wall of the Frisco Mint
—Emperor Norton I owe you a dollar for saying "Frisco" now I
  owe you two—
unveiling a sleepwalker's handprint
long out of circulation, not to be
outdone by the ocean, and tomorrow the sun
will one-up the moon!
Crazy things are bound to go down.
That earthquake off the coast of Chile (spitting frog)
. . . another off the coast of Japan . . . (red tamale)
I guess the earthquakes are running on fumes
A butterfly knife in the gelato shop

it's gonna get sticky
but we'll be safe in our animal masks and glitter.

Everyone on Ocean Beach seemed slightly dazed
by the intensity of the waves, the way the sun blazed
through dark clouds bordering mile-deep rivers of pale blue
where more pale, possibly younger
clouds crept like clods of seafoam on the jellied sand

I scooped some up and found it made
other foam I'd ever held myself come across green
as high school sweethearts lie in a field with flash bulbs in their eyes
and strange marks on their throats
when it flew off my fingers in little shreds
right onto Cedar's fleece windbreaker

Such opulence!

I wanted to drive to Sutro's mansion
to see empty pedestals
and tour the mintgreen ruins,
magic tourists.
Sutro was a rich man

his spiked money
a slippery civic ball
anyone who wants can kick.
Breath can kick.
Once he's lain there long enough
a rich man's grave becomes his spa
where all competition, anxiety
about status, the insanity expected of you
melts in your chops
dripping over your brain
like clarified butter
in an awestruck glow.

It's Saturday night, big night for going out.

I'm going to sleep all night, but first I'm going
to write some poems. I love writing poems.

This is the Bay Bridge.
An incredible, gray
rip on all the little red

taillights spilt down her
lowcut
evening dress. Beautiful

Bride! the bridge is
                laughing, touching her
throat
her fingernails
painted the color of the endpapers of
The Collected Haiku of the SFPD

Everyone's going out tonight

What about all the beetles in the dirt on the cliff above

Yes—what about them?
makes me a poet
writing the poem
One way to know you're in love
—Brazen Felicity—
they'd eat me up if I slept in

they'd sew my flesh
into little coats for flowers,

growing all over everything,
with their shiny pincers

(somberly or not)

I forgot all about those bugs till I gave you a ride
You were telling me a dream, city sprawling
I was walking through the outskirts of your voice
still spinning
the wheel: I was
the outskirts
inside myself
your voice
twisted up in fish silvers
hovering above the tracks
with moon gumption.

the thing is to say what's going on in
your own way

to be natural. That's true

otherwise. There is no such place

you're the only spectacle for me

people say poems are dirty
they're only as dirty as your face

DRUNKARD'S ALMANAC

When I'm drunk I'm a communard
making a whirlwind
tour of the minarets
having marathon conversations
with beautiful women
getting a captive audience
off on a technicality
I take the 5th
and uphold it
I meet the heads of state
and run off with their air guitars
Noon finds me curbside
with the Whore of Babylon
whoever
s/he is
I attend the double marriage
of identical twins
on my extra-tall camel
and dripping with irony
skinnydip with smooth space

aliens of alarming sobriety
Jean-Luc Godard
kiss me I'm a communard
and I swear
by the angelic clothespin
choir of tenements
and the plovers
of drastic autonomy
not to hurt the kids

EXISTENTIALIST SPA

I think I'd like to take a shot
at living in the sea
or, like Beckett, bite it
in French. Only
my French is abysmal
so I foresee limitations in that direction
Translate this
snarl the gangsters of translation
—but as I pass the window
of the men's shop and my reflection
flips trans-
parent like the pelican
on driftglass,
I tip my hat to the squares:
I guess I want to start
over, and in the same
breath think again.
Never seen myself as a
man exactly,
never knew you cared

And something else:
I'd like to be world famous
at least once before I die
but don't want to kill anyone,
so how?
I despise myself a little
in the mirror of this swank place,
just another rumor spread by
slummers,
and I'm sick of all these potshots
at the bourgeoisie—
Jean-Paul Sartre I'm talkin' to you!

GARDENS & AIRPLANES

balmy today
the high gray clouds
have no definition
an airplane slightly more
pronounced makes its way
sotto voce over the
spurs of the
Santa Cruz mountains pale
green where the full
meaning of spring has not been
discovered only
intimated.
The old woman discovers a new
rose and names it Kubrick
—that's why she's a poet—
and the dead cat in the round-
about is nothing but
a paper bag
the hedgerows keep
coming like a flight

simulator keeps ordering
ice cream floats
bare-assed
Lancelot has to hop and pop
wine skins with his forehead
bwyou   you   you
I want to be almost not there too
a lot less than a dream is,
peach flecked wide white petals
joined by a button of dragon tooth
here and gone
what isn't?
still

THE COMMODITY SINGS TO ITS BELOVED

I am here
for a very particular reason:
to buy a 6-pack of beer
and berries out of season

all for you, i did it all for you

I noticed an oil spill
on my drive past the bay,
emergency broadcast on the radio
—What do you have to say?

all for you, i did it all for you

You chopped down the plant
that used to grow my pants,
resurrected it in Indonesia
like a blow-up doll with amnesia

all for you, i did it all for you

Poor people once lived here
but you flooded the valley
with psilocybin carcinogens,
and forced the kids into shooting galleries

all for you, i did it all for you

You gave poor people jobs
then you forced them to act
like robots lining up
for a real live heart attack,
made them take apart their futures
then you sold the parts back,
repurposed the sutures
to close a robocaller's rap

all for you, i did it all for you

You got children in slums
to make things that break,
your unspoken credo—
"If it lasts, it's fake."

But you were there first
when we were dying of thirst,
with a pint of chilled water
each, for me, my wife and two daughters,

and even a kewpie doll
and a tiny stuffed puppy
—for my wife some paper slippers,
for me, a stuffed yuppie

—You saw every decision
that I would make first,
and you did get there first
when we were dying of thirst

every decision
i make is part yours,
every step i take,
i take on your floor

You mangled my fingers,
polluted my streams,
screamed in my face,

closed deals over my dreams

all for you, i did it all for you

(and now it fades out,

"The Commodity Sings to its Beloved" song.

They'll say it was a good idea
done wrong
—"They should have got a bigger budget,
done it as a singalong.")

HEAVY LOSSES, BOSS

I am the sole owner of a long brass fence in this life.
I don't pretend to own men, I let them pretend.
My riches extend
to bottlecap mines, I tune the pine tree ruby.
Gold stomachers
and white doubloons,
my initials dance on a gold spittoon.
Dungeness claws leaf my crude for the secret,
I pay them to keep it.
This is my will.
When I die recycle me in Chinatown,
I want to come back a Chinaman in a long silk gown,
but fat as ever, fat
as ever.
Dissembled in the ground the tourists glaze—
the sheep are on the highway in the haze,
my yacht is on the harbour.
My kingdom for a link of ardour,
I loved a girl,
she had great legs.

Skeleton bonanzas sipping dregs,
my speculations
rendered by spiders—
would that the chaste dancer would kiss my neck.
Despair became regret,
a half-ounce note on the Pony Express,
last ditches for the west.
I ran the room in empty flesh,
they said they could taste the kid on my breath.
My cummerbund was satin Lethe,
the chandelier of horse's tears—often challenged me to remember
where
I'd got it.
But on fishing trips I drank canned beer,
keeping real, keeping real.
White flies on auto wrecks,
silver pudding from broken necks,
I gazed upon the slow decay of fire trucks in ocean spray,
gawked at slums,
the whorls on their hard-won thumbs
and conditions.
To be a squid in a shipwreck's kitchen,
to glow at the head like a miner! I

would have closed my shoe factory in China,
moved it to Missouri
—twin of the impossible.
My lynching days are over,
I steel queens on gallows
and catch their haloes.
I've got a knack for horseshoes,
I catch the dollar jumping
and burn it in a pumpkin.
For this I'm Honcho
Hollow, I grin and caterpillars follow.
I keep a man to shine my fence,
Eliot's his name,
shining fences is his game.
But when the Big One hit he vanished down a water main.
I was standing there like a sucker holding the broken chain,
—I watched my mansion fall,
my heir bum change,
Enrico sang to Teddy in a bath house on the cliff,
he sang
"My favorite soldier has no brain"
with a wet towel round his neck.
I found it

sick, but I was too late.
Sturm and Drang skipped naked through the trees,
twin sisters with nipples bit raw.
The stars in the sky were comprehensively detached,
the sheep went Ba, Ba.
And my wife couldn't pull the snails off her eyes—
we went native in the Big Lie like spies on the Peninsula.
I had my elephant gun
and a map of Bombay with gutters that moved.
I shot on sight, brought down a kite
with a fiver for a tail.
And I rebuilt my fortune on that snail,
rung up Eliot in a leaking pail,
went to see the elephant with Jack London and Ishmael—
I dropped my pants at the mouth of Hell.
Neons
burned like race horses in the rain,
and my boy came home in uniform
with a
bandaged face
and a plastic leg. I ordered a keg.
Here's my will.
There's nothing left on the chicken but a farm.

Fine crystal equilibrium on the Holdings,
tune it in the dark.
I vaguely recall being drunk in a park
and sleeping under the news I'd made.
The pain sets in when you remove the blade.
To be a printer's ap-
prentice by trade!
or a scantily clad kickboxer in a video game arcade,
I would have gambled,
I would have paid.

EGYPTIAN BOWLING TROPHY

Doug Hitler
        —not a name
likely to open many doors—
meditates
on the chill, ancient coin:

Those aren't prosthetic
feathers you see—
they irrigate his knuckles . . .
Evolution
can be torture

The Pharoah   fell off his surfboard

                Velour evolved a soul

Few knew
  but those few
    made up a who's who
      of who knew

how low can you go?
low as Doug

really low because I really want to go low.

THERE'S LOVE AND THEN THERE'S LOVE

In the shady
        palm your brain
matures
from ectoplasm to manure
green to brown clock
            high in your skull
doves
    feed their chicks
on soft newspaper twists
shot w/ hot straw
                echoed from yr
                    barnyard.
O yr grace
        gleams in the quicksilver
        gossip of stewardesses
                    and stews
        in the top hats of mayors.
You are so much more than
a regular undergraduate—
As your bag comes off

the conveyer the sky clears
to white + blue steps:
"Imhotep" you whisper
"was the first to see the escalator
in a grain of sand."
—And then the bags go faster
and faster until they crash
and burn,
and a redwing blackbird
steps from the canvas—
He's your spirit animal and
he's smashed on nectar,
imperious baron
of the airwaves,
wingin' o'er the wastes of
                    the duchy.
West-Village living
and so much pain and
          theft in the cards, only
a perfect poem will get you off
                          As you drift
on your evening rounds to the soul
stylings of the Mad Lads

waxed on yr inner ear: Something
more than *American Psycho*
rings out on the street
hot with the latest from Gettysburg
and you, in your grasshopper raincoat
sound the high note—

Milk! Milk!

and Kool-Aid L'eggs—
crossed muskets and wolf milk,
O come all ye beggars
befoibled and lumpen—
hot milk floods the valleys of the sky!

ZERO WITH A THOUSAND ACES

Let's you and I lose
touch a million times, let's lose
every last bit of touch
till
I'm in Rome and you're in
Christ.
Mother glass don't come btwn
us—I'll make a scene
to honor you.
What's the last time
the paparazzi wrestled an
octopus
    in a glade of lips?
We'll slip out
and walk on water.
It's all relative.
The world's supposed to be so
big
    to the wild boars of
Chernobyl,

but then
the night which chases all a-
round
can feel so confidential
—in stories of mistaken identity
+ comic resolution
—in the high/low swap
(Prince and Pauper
Hal + Falstaff
Scheherazade's
forced perspective)
it's esp. perspicacious, maybe
b/c the night too
is double: the genuine
intruder
always finds herself
stuck in an intolerably stupid
drama / until he's beheaded
Mussolini
asleep is no
less malignant than
Mussolini awake.
When do you walk away?

When sing?
What business do poets have
even voting? I mean
in poem, what is "vote"?
Cut the bastard's throat
clean through—
True story:
his statue still stands
in the elephant moat
of outer Rome
—the Ethiope Rimbaud.

MOVE ON

One night I was trying to think of something
nice to write about, and I thought
of you, and how you'd stolen my heart,
and though you put it right back
way back when—how it's still missing
a beat out of each minute.
I thought of how happy I was being near you,
how I once put my head on your lap
and you stroked my hair
with your fingertips.
It might be disgusting, but I didn't really care
about sleeping with you—
I wouldn't say no. I mean,
my fuzziness was the whole problem, wasn't it?
Why wasn't I more insistent?
If we'd died five million years ago
on a bed of hot ash,
archaeologists would conclude
women were bigger than men back then,
and just as long as our broken leg bones crossed
I wouldn't mind.

INNER OAF

There is an oaf in my
body
trying to get out

Ever since I ran straight
into that
tether pole
in 5th grade
I have been possessed
of a wicked oaf

An oaf entered my body
when I fell flat on my face
in front of the death squad
and fled
when I blew Christ
a kiss

I will never let him go—
I'm afraid
he might hurt himself
or hurt
those closest to him
with the weapon
of his oafishness

PIERRE DE RONSARD

My sweet youth is gone
My strong shoots cracked
I've got a white key and a black tooth
My nerves dissolve at a touch
And my veins (cold leads)
Run wine in place of blood.
    Take this lyre, little girl
All my great loves writhe in those strings
Even you—I sense we're near the end
Nothing kills youth faster
Than getting old slowly
With one match, a bed and a bottle.
    Someone should hang me and stuff my head—
Too many years and sicknesses—
Like everyone else, right next to death
The whole time—And I thought it was different
With me! Well just as long as I'm not late—
Give the living my regards.
    What right do I have after all, at this
Late hour, to loiter or demur?

All I know is the barkeeper's the Devil
Or one of them—He always welcomed me
Oh yes he kept his door open very wide—
And to keep from returning I never left!

THE PERFECT MAN

FOR KAILEY

He comes from the age of gasoline
        His mother was a beauty queen
His pecs bedazzle unto spheres
        One fan was Lady Windermere
He'll poach your egg and make it snappy
        Produce your kid and change the nappy
His IQ's 182
        He belongs with Chomsky in the zoo
And yet he sees himself as little
        More than an air on God's flatfooted fiddle
—Music to your ears, and those alone
        The man of the hour, he's your dog to the bone
He looks like Sting in 1974
        In a sharkskin suit on the dancehall floor
He'll fuck you hard until you come
        Then suck your cunt 'til your asshole's numb
He long ago gave up politics
        For a frozen Blaxploitation Buddhist kick

He knows the Left is another religion
Just like the dove is a kind of pigeon
And he trembles in Parisian skies
Scarfs Berliners with Cold War spies,
Shakespeare apes, and Barthes recites
On a green grass track through the warp of night
He knows the law, and where to bend it
The case for indifference, and how to defend it

THE RED CAPS

a poem on Kailey's birthday

Puce dumpster, rust in dew

Waterworks of black bamboo,
Ticonderoga pencil snap
on a divan of crystallized sap

Inside some young bark lacquered pine

desktops arm for drool,
the one-track minded ax
took its cut then learned to relax

A little French would go here nicely,
I'd mouth it in a trance so princely
to the symbiosis of the woodpecker and the diamond bongo
—*comment ça va dire?*

It does not matter,
the moon floats like a soapbar on the sky, which splashes
and licks the feral rooftops of Paris
till its rope is ghostly

It stings when it gets in your eye,
but this sting insures its numbing cure
in the diagonal roadwork of bats

in the bangles of a captive dancing sun

She evolved that circumspection
of lightning timing and misdirection
worthy of an evaporating scarecrow

to make hay, and smear the night with green and gold paint

Expressly to revisit
illicit desolation, both past and fast approaching

11-27-14

MOUCHE VERTE MORTE

mouche verte morte
au rayon du soleil
deniché
—tout comme la babouche
du soldat de plomb
—regarde ses guêtres écaillées,
ses vertèbres
embouties
sur son dos
incliné
comme il dodeline
la tête
au bord du lit de plume

les ailes se réveillent—
le soldat est facteur—
en se regardant . . .
le pantalon plissé—

GREEN BOTTLE FLY

fly green dead
            in a bolt of sun
                unearthed
—like a slipper
                    for the tin soldier
—look at his spattered shins,
            backbone
                    pressed tin
        on his back
slope
as he nods
            his head
at the edge of the feather bed

            wings awake—
soldier is mailman—
        looks himself over . . .
white slacks with the crease—

lettres pour rire
pour femmes
    qui pleurent

toy letters
for real
    crying women

LOUIS ARMSTRONG INTERNATIONAL

The full-bodied women on the plane
were harbingers of the full-bodied
women at Ewan's wedding
but Esther, who I talked to
for an hour about—what?
was skinny and bespeckled
like me!—and lovely, too.
In the cab I (this morning)
see some of her in Marie-Claude
from Montreal (not really her name).
Flirting is fun . . . "In
another life / or a slightly
different one . . . " Or not.
Auntie April's lemon meringue
would still be here, still blowing
my socks off. But it's like
this—we cobble our mutual
intelligence together, let our
good points cancel each other
out and see what's left—

that's the good stuff. I
don't tell her that tomorrow
I'll be just another asshole
writing a lighthearted poem
on the toilet in Louis Armstrong
International—she seems to get it.

BERKELEY VOICE NOTES

On my walk there is a palm tree
furred feral and sorta senile

Sorta cute and lonely
like a desert wallflower

Like a Bedouin Yeti
whose real life is forgotten

After a string of summer blockbusters dramatize his struggle

Cold rapids must rush
over the moon to make it glow so

Where rails gathered
the Key Line once performed its naïve pirouette

Scales in spring air
an Oakland eye doctor's daughter
plays them

plays them again

Man she's thorough
the night is narrow

A flour handprint on her apron

St. Joseph approves
St. Joseph is so hip!

with his T-square and his stone cheeks
while the automatic sprinklers fizzle

We enter the broad walk
close eyes and accelerate

Powder-pink bricks
the virgin pipes cross their fingers

Under the lawn-statue Buddha
more holy for its cheapness

Turquoise Mardi Gras beads
at the tip of the hose

That garden hose nose
really goes to your head

Consult the bunny tablets
in Buddha's lap

Make love to your mom's soulmate
grow up absurd

Live the truth
what choice is there?

*

I spent all night with a stuffed shirt

Turtle dove in a fern tree

Falcon '65

See, I'm retracing my steps

I'm under the magnolia tree again

There is the choice again

Smoke drifts from the pink bong

and then a hand jumps out and grabs you by the throat!

Zapatista with a leaf blower

achieves lift-off

Tai chi club on the basketball court at dawn

Full court press!

I'm reading these words in a pamphlet at the window
one of those beautiful windows
you crank like a tent

The calico kitten
the turtle dove
and the hot boy in brown wingtips

All go past my window

They seem to be each other
            at different points in the story

Am I the plot?

*

I'll pretend to be a Hollywood actor,
a real star,
and why don't you be the journalist
who is responsible for telling my story?

But I can't walk down the street
without little white butterflies landing on my hot dog,
so we've gotta talk
in the locked planetarium.

Am I starting to tremble?
Don't let them tell you I don't tremble anymore.

There's something going on
between us.

Something off-the-record.

INDEPENDENTLY BLUE

It's easy to fly a flag when you live in a nice house
in a beautiful city.
Things have worked out nicely for you,
and you think everyone can agree
this is the greatest country on earth.
The Bay Area is full of hikers with portfolios.
Goggles in German skycar ride my ass past the prison.
The day they break that prison down
to a funhouse, and the rapists to mirrors,
I'll fly a flag.
I've never seen a bum pushing a shopping cart with a flag sticking
    out
of his can, but I'm not saying that doesn't exist.
This is America, after all.

IF YOU'RE READING THIS

it means everything turned out OK.
Nuclear war was averted,
environmental catastrophe, too.
Light up a big joint and congratulate yourself.
Your mother and I were so worried.
But there is another possibility:

That you're reading this at gunpoint
because the Chinese have taken back California,
or
that you picked this up at random
from a library
full of corpses:
you don't understand a word you're
reading, you're
dead and these words are being
read over your body before
they shove your flag-draped
coffin into the Gulf—actually
these aren't even the words being read.
But the chances are slim.

It's much more likely
that Disaster has been locked up
in a coniferous hospital
ward, like the bogeyman,
and the unmade moonlit beds
are the headstones of our nightmares.
Everything turned out fine,
and I'm standing eye-to-eye with you
in a broad, clean public park
having escaped
at 43.

REAL-LIFE ADVENTURE

About a group of poets and artists living close together
as the world goes crazy and they go crazy
with each other, getting into fights and driving
each other crazy but maintaining a precise
order that keeps switching but is always
precise. I am one of them.
My poems are incredible, I write all the time
when I'm not doing more important things:
it's the most important thing I do
after being all there for my kids, maybe making a little
more money than last month, sleeping
with my wife and eating with her and walking in the hills
with her, getting drunk from time to time and writing
these incredible poems sober and dizzy free—
and the group ends up changing the whole story of art
and poetry and inspiring other groups and young
kids. A great vibrant striving, an absurdity
a tender absurdity held in place—in the
art and the poems. A silly pointless urging in
a world without a place to go, and all of us

jamming and spinning off each other in the city
and up on the farm growing our own food, twisting
our own pretzels and printing our own things and rush-
ing it out to the thriving rival scenes while
war and chaos and greed tear the world apart
and everyone is going crazy one way or the other
—restoring the sweet ambling adventure to the whole span,
the whole needless disaster flipped on a whim of bright
bread, broken. And one night
I'm reading Blake in bed in the big nursery
and everyone's asleep except someone in the green-
house, and I can hear low voices from the press
room, too . . . and I've got a lamp on my page
—*Songs of Innocence, Songs of Experience*—
and there are stairs at my head going up
and more at my feet going down
to the new moon in the glass V with the three tall
trees above the highway
and the ocean—is that overdoing it?—and
I get it, reading Blake, lying there
in a kid's box bed
since there's guests tonight, guests and guests:
that I'm just one small person in this big group, one

poet about to write a poem that may
or may not be so incredible, one more mouth
to feed, one chewing nattering mouth—
a really famous happy poet who people love
to hear read, who takes the train
to the city and people buy me drinks and laugh
and laugh and hug me
among heralds at the barricades.

THIS IS THE LIFE

Maybe I'm fooling myself about this
aristocracy of artists thing,
and maybe it's a little stuck up
to number myself among them
but it makes me feel
better—to assume a 3rd reality
is thriving in secret channels
all thru the planet, gearing
up for its showdown
with naked hairy politics.

Any optimist today makes an
absurdist under black light
and the deeper you get the fatter
your fine bones grow, the
grislier the hunt the more el-
egant the symbols—O to be
gobsmacked and fiercely art-
iculate all at once! to die
truly hip, and for the book

I leave behind
to be handy as a magnum
of the driest champagne
with the tiniest bubbles
for washing down the raw flesh
of the ruling class.

Ahhh!

SILVER TO SILVER

Why are you writing a book?
they ask me. My book discusses courage and
tells a story. It is about friendship.
What else can I do? I've stopped looking
for perfection, now I'm looking
for Russian epaulets. I want naked bodies
that trust each other. Here I'm turning
my words into images. I'm not exemplary since
to be exemplary would be to be consistent.
Well, I'm not, I'm in love.

The state of the world calls out for poetry to save it. LAWRENCE FERLINGHETTI

CITY LIGHTS SPOTLIGHT SHINES A LIGHT ON THE WEALTH OF INNOVATIVE AMERICAN POETRY BEING WRITTEN TODAY. WE PUBLISH ACCOMPLISHED FIGURES KNOWN IN THE POETRY COMMUNITY AS WELL AS YOUNG EMERGING POETS, USING THE CULTURAL VISIBILITY OF CITY LIGHTS TO BRING THEIR WORK TO A WIDER AUDIENCE. IN DOING SO, WE ALSO HOPE TO DRAW ATTENTION TO THOSE SMALL PRESSES PUBLISHING SUCH AUTHORS. WITH CITY LIGHTS SPOTLIGHT, WE WILL MAINTAIN OUR STANDARD OF INNOVATION AND INCLUSIVENESS BY PUBLISHING HIGHLY ORIGINAL POETRY FROM ACROSS THE CULTRUAL SPECTRUM, REFLECTING OUR LONGSTANDING COMMITMENT TO THIS MOST ANCIENT AND STUBBORNLY ENDURING FORM OF ART.

CITY LIGHTS SPOTLIGHT

1

Norma Cole, *Where Shadows Will: Selected Poems 1988–2008*

2

Anselm Berrigan, *Free Cell*

3

Andrew Joron, *Trance Archive: New and Selected Poems*

4

Cedar Sigo, *Stranger in Town*

5

Will Alexander, *Compression & Purity*

6

Micah Ballard, *Waifs and Strays*

7

Julian Talamantez Brolaski, *Advice for Lovers*

8

Catherine Wagner, *Nervous Device*

9

Lisa Jarnot, *Joie de Vivre: Selected Poems 1992–2012*

10

Alli Warren, *Here Come the Warm Jets*

11

Eric Baus, *The Tranquilized Tongue*

12

John Coletti, *Deep Code*

13

Elaine Kahn, *Women in Public*

14

Julien Poirier, *Out of Print*

15

David Brazil, *The Holy Ghost & Other Poems*